C0-ARP-881

3 2711 00140 4437

LONG LIVE
A HUNGER
TO FEED
EACH OTHER

ENTERED FEB 2 1 2008

Also by Jerome Badanes

The Final Opus of Leon Solomon

...MBIA COLLEGE LIBRARY
600 S. MICHIGAN AVENUE
CHICAGO, IL 60605

LONG LIVE
A HUNGER
TO FEED
EACH OTHER

POEMS BY JEROME BADANES

INTRODUCTION BY NANCY WILLARD

OPEN CITY BOOKS

New York

Copyright © 2007 Gail Kinn

Published by permission of the University of Michigan,
Special Collections Library, Jerome Badanes Papers

All rights reserved, including the right of reproduction in
whole or in part in any form.

Printed in the United States of America

Design by Nick Stone

These poems have previously appeared in the following
publications: "Enkidu from the Underworld, Remembering His
Life," *Generation*; "From Day to Day" and "A Burning Coal,"
Hanging Loose; "A Darkness Between Us," *Michigan Quarterly
Review*; lines from a number of poems were printed together
under the title "Long Live a Hunger to Feed Each Other,"
CAW! An additional eight poems appeared in
Blood and *Landscapes*.

Library of Congress Control Number: 2007924108
ISBN-10: 1-890447-46-3
ISBN-13: 978-1-890447-46-5

OPEN CITY BOOKS
270 Lafayette Street
New York, NY 10012
www.opencity.org

07 08 09 10 11 12   10 9 8 7 6 5 4 3 2 1

CONTENTS

Photograph by Eric Lindbloom

Jerome Badanes in 1980

INTRODUCTION

Ten years after Jerome Badanes died on a May morning in 1995 on his way to teaching his writing class at Sarah Lawrence, I was asked to speak about poetry to a group of writers at Columbia, and during the discussion, a subject came up that sometime in their lives all poets ask themselves: What makes a poem last?

I thought of a spring day in Manhattan in 1965, when Jerry took several friends for a walk across the Brooklyn Bridge and paused to point out the last fourteen lines of his long narrative poem "From Brooklyn to Manhattan on the D Train" he had penciled on the surface of a girder.

I whistle across water at Brooklyn Bridge.
Birds burst from my lips toward Brooklyn Bridge.
The setting sun hums on Brooklyn Bridge.
The horizon is an orchard there are camels
loaded with libraries donkeys
bearing melons and apples and grapefruit
an old lady giving birth to an orange and who
but a few poets and for one second some suicides
and a man lame with love to build that bridge?
And my throat is hoarse with such a need to shout
Look at that bridge just look at it!

The old buildings are blinking with proverbs.
Beauty is slitting to a close above us.
We vacuum back into darkness oh creature!

It was a poem I remembered well from hearing him read it in a loft in Soho. The rain that inspires poems does not save them, and a few weeks later the rain had washed away these words from the gunmetal surface on which he wrote them. But what vanishes from our sight lives on in us when we are haunted by poems. For those of us who were privileged to know Jerry and hear him read, his poems are a lens through which we see our own lives as stops on a journey that connects all of us. To this day, when I stand with my suitcase on the platform of the Poughkeepsie train station and listen for the overnight train bound for Detroit and points west, I hear Jerry's voice in these lines from "A Journey by Rail Through the Night." He is telling me about the old woman who sat next to him on that same journey, thirty years before, but the number of years do not matter, for when I read the poem the journey is always new:

We're flying above the train
the two of us. There's a chill
in the air tonight our
cheeks are laughing.
The train shrinks
its flat clap and a cough dissolves is
gone
we're alone
with the re-emerging rasping of the crickets
the hush of prairie grasses and leaves
light-
years gone
on the moon lighted planet America.

Like Galway Kinnell and William Carlos Williams, Badanes understood the art of packing the sounds and signs of the American landscape into a long poem, and haunted by Whitman's generous voice, he was on his way to finding his own place in American poetry. When Williams wrote, in Book II of *Paterson*, "What do I do? I listen . . . This is my entire occupation" he might have been speaking for Badanes, whose ear for the poignance and humor shining just under the skin of ordinary speech shapes his poems. Seldom has a poet taken that advice as seriously as Badanes did when he was interviewing Holocaust survivors for the 1981 documentary film, "Image Before My Eyes" and found himself haunted by their voices.

In the seventies Badanes's political involvement in the antiwar movement turned him away from writing poetry to writing for and performing in street theatre, and finally to writing fiction, from which emerged, many years later, his major work, a novel of the Holocaust published by Knopf, *The Final Opus of Leon Solomon*. In the brief interview that accompanied Edith Milton's *New York Times* review, Badanes commented on these changes. "You get wised up to leave your own roots and then you get wiser— you return." At the time of his death he was at work on a second novel, *Change or Die*.

This volume of Badanes's poetry, which he himself assembled, invites you to meet the artist as a young man through the poems he wrote from 1962 to 1975.

Timeless and haunting, they stand on their own.

—Nancy Willard
Vassar College

A JOURNEY BY RAIL THROUGH THE NIGHT

My insides
reel
with God's blizzard outside
as *The Wolverine* fogs by at four A.M.
The insulated coach is warm
an old woman her
mouth opened
sucking
her head
bent to my shoulder
beside me sleeps
as we edge through Armageddon in *Black Rock*.

I sniff her tottering heart's tick
and feel against my hips her
storage sacks slowly filling up.
Miles behind my back my child
sleeps in a room I cannot see.
Do lights sweep across the ceiling?
Do cats slip back and
forth across the woodwork?
Do cancers bounce on the skylight?
Her mother is there too but I

can't remember her except
for an immense smile somehow like tears.

I light a cigarette and think
of a Greyhound bus driver with a
powerful neck north
on the California coast
Pacific and Sierra.
The stars clamor above us and
my small orange light sizzles
back from the dark bus.
The driver is beautiful and monstrous.
Everyone else is asleep.

The conductor grunts by.
Her head trembles backward and loses ground.
"Where oh where are we?"
"Entering Canada, ma'm. Are you comfortable?"
"Trains are trains."
Stoically, she rejoins her body.

The train eats through Canada.

Mouthing through Canada is
Louis Armstrong.

He vacuums out sit
down you're rocking the boat.
Trumpets hump at my heart.
She snores. Her
heartbeat is a bass fiddle.
The loco-
motive whistle whistles
through my spine my bowels burn.
Dreams. Poet Father Lover Jesus Christ
Louis Armstrong Jesus Christ Old Lady!
how are you seventy-five years old?
how do you play on that trumpet?
And bum
I gave you milk
the panacea white milk.
You clutched your container
of milk and asked me for words as
you had a question you couldn't handle.
How do you wake up?
Grandfather
run-a-round atheist cantor
who sucked the juice at dawn
from eggs through pinholes
then put them back
for your family's nourishment and
woke them up marvelous baritone bird!

How dead granddaddy do
I sing through
synagogues and hum to myself?

We're flying above the train
the two of us. There's a chill
in the air tonight our
cheeks are laughing.
The train shrinks
its flat clap and a cough dissolves is
gone
we're alone
with the reemerging rasping of the crickets
the hush of prairie grasses and leaves
light-
years gone
on the moon lighted planet America.

Louis Armstrong
wipes his brow in West Berlin
grandfather rubs noses with ammonia.
But for us
old woman it was
in the stars so don't fret. Look
you're as young
as mother's favorite photograph

on the boat coming over steerage
in a fluttering summer smock
as if not grandmother but
Valentino himself
were saying smile my angel to you.
Besides
didn't you always
want
to fly through the air?
Give me your hand.
Look at the trees the rows
of trees to block the wind
so the wheat may grow
peacefully and bread
be bountiful on our tables.
Give me your hand. We'll
glide and
caper two wayfaring
kites
our tails entwined
the bees in their
rapture will have
nothing on us. Woman
the world's asleep in a tube
wake up
my small breathing daughter the

teddy bears are on strike
lines of them
with signs you throw us out too
soon we protest.
Woman
why are there offices why
are train seats one
behind the other we all look
forward all night long
at silhouettes cut in glass
or sleep? Mother
we are two kites father

come join us
you are sixty-four years old
and you never walked on water will
I ever walk on water?
Will I be crouched in this chair
and make notations of five o'clock
as you lean from a ladder thirty forty fifty
years?

The kites gambol the boys
all afternoon their feet
planted
on the edges of high buildings

sense in their fingers
the tug
of America's weather
the serious
freedom of the kites.
Small children
peg stones at each other
mothers fry the smells
seep
in
all night
pigeons sniffed at my liver.

"Wake up
young man
soon we stop
in Detroit but
the snow is
smiling to us.
Wake up."
Because
of your chattering husband's
ineptitude your son's
viciousness the
flour mill
burned down with

all your icons and warmth.
Your back is a man's back your
men are puppies your
grandson departs
you will never
touch him
again. He waves to you a simple
movement.

"Once I kissed
and kissed again each
of those small fingers!"

Her tiredness
weighing on the pier
she waves back
with a final benediction.
Smokestacks bellow birds
gyre from sleep
the big boat
edges by.
Behind
its slender scalloping shadow dawn
swings slowly out.
With her old woman's
heavy voice

she talks to God
saying
"the world is so wonderful!"

Good morning! my beautiful old crone.

GUINEA-GOLDEN

The dime sticks to my palm and glitters
as I whirl to the sun of bay seven.

Small girls spiral tricky castles
along the great Atlantic Ocean.
Their mothers,
backed by umbrellas, bellies
nudging the horizon,
or some, on World War II army blankets,
their backs unhooked to the sun,
watch the young men's
body building calesthenics in the sand.

My mother dishes spaghetti from a jar
and says, "eat your lunch,
before you lose that dime."
I sit in the sand and fill my mouth
with spaghetti and chew
through lumps and lumps of it.
Grits of sand chill my teeth
and the white sun bakes my nose.

I watch the seagulls
washing their white wobbly appetites
and long to flap my arms
and strut like a seagull, or a commando,
and dip my nose in the water
and rinse my mouth,
split the waves like a P.T. boat,
sub-machine-gun my gallop to the beach
and inspire the driftwood to follow.
"No swimming for a half hour, you just ate."

I bite down on the dime and scoop
a narrow hole in the beach until
I feel wet earth
between my fingers, and twitch
with the image of black beetles.
Then I bomb the dime in, bury it,
and memorize the place
by where the lifeguard lounges,
and, for insurance,
I squeeze a bottle cap in,
on top, and leave to scout the sea.

I spout like a whale and think
I'm a submarine
sneaking through waves for a better look

at the fortified castles manned
by amazons who will, if they spot me,
cut my fingers off,
scalp me,
bury me to my neck in the sand,
and dance without clothes around me
until the tide comes in.

My cold thighs burn
and my shriveled groin
feels warm and silly against the cold sand.

Jerome the pirate-marine
from Gibraltar and Guadalcanal
With a knife in my teeth and the gold earring jangling,
with boots and a purple heart,
with Iwo Jima bursting in me,
with silence, dripping wet, I storm the beach,
sidestep beer bottles and bones,
dazzle the ladies, careful
for the yellow ju-jitsu jungle fighters
behind umbrellas and baskets.

"Mama, hurry, the treasure."

I guide her safely beyond
lifeguard lookout. There's
the secret cap. I kick it off.
I scoop the sand.
Everyone is watching, the queens in their towers,
the young men through their muscles.
The hole is deep.
My fingernails are bloody with beetles.

JANUARY, 1944

The party had begun. Pressing against
the wooden bars until eyes were almost to the kitchen,
forehead strained to the pinched and drained laughter
of the women. I remember the laughter

sifting through colors of confetti
and the loud voices of the men were like
aeroplanes and frogs. My five years trilled
in a crib to my parent's tenth Anniversary party.

Irving Lipmann, famous for tangos, boomed
on the glasses and lightbulbs until the slats shook.
His eyes were diamonds and a face so red
(from fishbones and beer) he seemed deeper

than President Roosevelt.
Feet sliding to the sides he led them,
hands to each other's shoulders, one by one to the end
where Gellerman, who always pinched me with fingers

as strong and as straight as his pipe,
bent everyone forward and kicked back from the knees.
They danced around the dining-room table
into the parlor and back, shouting

"whathe hell do we care
the gang's all here . . . whathe hell do we care . . ."
The dining-room table was stretched
with chopped foods cut foods keyboards of glasses,

weenies and turkey wings and tottering bottles.
The glass top would surely have broken
but Papa had put it safely, silently, with me.
The same cool glass that turned ceilings into floors.

I used to look down into it and cool my chin.
The floor was white and vague
and the doorways, upside-down, had ledges
I longed to climb over.

It was Gellerman who plucked me from bed. While
    father smiled,
from Lipmann to Swirsky to Spiewak
to Gellerman I shrieked on the ends of their laughter
the confetti blazing in my face.

Until my mother led me back.
Then to bed with murmurs heard
from another world, the parlor world, lulling
to sleep a child curled warmly about a mother's word.

ENKIDU FROM THE UNDERWORLD, REMEMBERING HIS LIFE (for M. J. Benardete)

Enkidu, who is both the subject and narrator of this poem, is a character in the ancient Babylonian *Epic of Gilgamesh*. Gilgamesh, the young king of the city of Uruk, is strong, handsome, wise, brave, foolhardy, and is resented by many people and many gods. So Enkidu is created full blown to be his equal and bring him down a peg. He lives on the steppes with the animals. He is hairy and strong. Since he opens traps and frightens hunters, it is decided that he must be lured to the city, and the temple prostitute is asked to do the luring. He goes to the city, fights with, and becomes brothers with, Gilgamaesh. They go on adventures together, but Enkidu has lost something, and slowly he dies.

—J. B.

Editor's note: This poem was never completed.

1.
Sensuous with animals and among mountains.
Centuries ago.
If I could remember it clearly I would speak of gazelles.
I would speak of my legs
and how my cheeks were jostled by sand
as I ran on the rims of streams and steppes
and bounced the bait of pale men
who grabbed at lions and wolves, like men.

But except that I did these things
it's hard to remember.
The harlot's lonely breasts pierced my chest.
We coupled until the loneliness and chill of it
became fat and slow and too much.
As if I drank full streams of cold water.

So I went back to the animals. The gazelles
twisted their bodies from streams I came laughing toward,
and like strange beasts ran off.
The lions roared from a distance
and slowly turned and slowly walked away.

Of all that happened to me I remember that best.
How the animals turned from me and my shoulders bent.
How my hairs became thin and dull

as the sunlight seeped out from the ends of them.
How my legs twitched and the hard ground became soft.
How in myself I was afraid.

I knew nothing then except that I was weak.
And my lust grew again for that woman,
and for her cities.

I returned to the woman and sat by her feet
and listened.
I looked in her face and listened.

She spoke of the strong city of Uruk,
of its young king Gilgamesh.
Gilgamesh, who with power of wild oxen, trampled
the privacy of husband and wife
and never slept at night.
I said lead me woman to the strong city of Uruk
and I will follow you.
I shouted I am Enkidu.
I am mighty. I was born on the steppes
and lived with the animals.
I am like a god.

Her eyelids tightened slightly.
She said:

"Come down to the city of Uruk.
There are women there,
and there are bright jewels and celebration and ease.
But, Enkidu, Gilgamesh is mightier than you.
The gods love him. Do not challenge him.

"And Gilgamesh awaits you. For he dreamt
that a large star
tumbled past his eyes as he slept
and fell by the city wall.
The people bent away from it and whispered.
And Gilgamesh bent toward it
as though to a woman."

At dawn she led me on the road to Uruk.
I made my step smaller to match the woman's
and my great shadow
continually nudged her smaller one.
I was delighted.

The woman's soft cloth
on my loins
was strange with the taste of her breasts.
We were dressed alike
as we walked on the wet grass.

And she knew her way to the sheepfolds.
Holding my hand
she led me to the place where shepherds eat.
Crowding closely to me, their foreheads creased,
they carefully looked
and then placed bread and strong wine at my feet.

But I,
who sucked the sweet milk from wild beasts,
what did I know of bread and deep wine
and swallowing?
The wine burnt my lips and my chin,
and the bread was clay on my tongue.

She said: "Enkidu, Enkidu, eat slowly.
Sip the wine." And her voice
softened my stare
as I ate and learned about men.

Seven . . . or was it twenty-three goblets,
or like the sheep who swayed and moved,
I couldn't count the wine I drank that day.

Then I was shepherd and huntsman
I rubbed their spice between my fingers and on my chest
and I clothed myself.
She said I was her long and handsome groom.
We laughed,
and I knew the heat of what she said.
And for my friends,
I took their sharp and pointed sticks
and caught and captured lions and wolves, like a man.

Though I shouted like a lion,
like a wolf, a gazelle, like a young boy,
and the twisting and the turning.
The leaves on all the trees bowed down
and the branches scraped my hair.

Laughter and words
mingled our bodies our eyes
until I felt so sweet and my eyes
so low so dark like the wine so warm
and the ground and the girl
—and a last quiet cheer from shepherds my friends.

A hero, I fell with my love and my arms,
and the brown leaves on the ground.

2.
One day
I tried to play the shepherd's pipe
but my hands became wet
and the shepherds laughed.

So I climbed into a tree
and slipped the pipe
over the tip of the highest branch,
and before I jumped down
I sang so loud
all the sheep at rest moved
like a field
on a still evening
when I sat by the stream
after drinking
watching as a small breeze came
and the field
like a single sleeping fish
in a still pond
shifted
and stayed sleeping.

And we laughed so hard then
that soon we became silent
listening to our bodies slowing down

and, after a while,
the breathing of the sheep in the quiet field
became our breathing too.

****

Night
and everyone was breathing
and the woman
like fallen leaves
after a long rain.
I would lie on my back
watching the moon moving across the sky slowly
though I never saw it move.
It was then I would think of Gilgamesh
and look both ways
and upon the woman sleeping.

Sometimes I would rub against her
and press her belly with my hand
and grip her head with my hand
and pull her sighing from sleep
and wrap her legs with mine
and make use of her
but not merrily
until I too was wet leaves

plopped back to the ground
on my back
and she
a lioness starving in a trap
until I fell asleep.

Other times I turned from her
and looked more at the moon
and spoke to it
as if it were Gilgamesh
and I would twist inside my body twisting
on the hard ground
and sometimes my body floated.

****

One day a man
with blotches on his face appeared
muttering in the sheepfolds.

I watched him squatting with the shepherds
who gave him wine and bread
and bent close to him when he talked

Standing up they turned toward me.
The shepherds pointed

and the man's head slowly moved
and I shouted:
I will go to the city of Uruk.
I will send Gilgamesh tumbling.

That same day
I started again on the road to Uruk,
The woman followed behind me
and I never looked back
except when she called
asking me to walk less quickly.

****

As the cold sun was setting
a pale moon wavered a moment in the sky.
Thick and rumbling slowly
like the back of an elephant stuffed in a pit
stood the strange city of Uruk.

Gray walls squatting in smoke
and the sounds of insects.
A city is covered with insects I thought
and my feet walked less quickly
and my heart fluttered
a gazelle trying to twist from my body and flee.

I could hear the people talking
but their words
were too quick or too many
and I, on heavy legs, looked straight out
and saw nothing.

Then there was silence
and I wished the buzzing would begin again
but the people stayed silent
and I was hot
and large as a camel as I walked between them.

Then one voice saying
"he is Gilgamesh to a hair,
not as tall but broader in the bones"
and I felt like a lion.
And a smaller voice,
"look he is hairy like a field"
and all the small people laughed
until the large people looked at them
and I felt like a sheep.
And I remembered the young shepherd
who said he would be as big and hairy as me someday
and I knew then that people die
as the animals die
because they start small

and become large
and lose their strength and their speed
and disappear in the same way.
Gazelles and lions and elephants and camels and people.

And I remembered
that when I approached the city
and the sun was falling toward darkness behind me
my shadow became longer and longer
and bobbed up on the wall and dissolved
into the smoke above.

FROM BROOKLYN TO MANHATTAN ON THE D TRAIN

We sniff each other's eyes slyly.
Like flowers
from the bellies of cut people the
taste of blood thickening my mouth I see
brotherhood
explode with the sour breath
from the sleeping assassin
of himself.

You! Mister Misery!
What buds break in your brain?
You! Drowsing Agent!
I see your one eye peeking.
And you you there you you you you you you
I mean you your eyes
they look like crutches and you
what blue skies make you thirsty?

You people slaughter my love.

Okay?
Okay triangle

(when our foreheads touch).
O creature
your nipples at my chest
kissing.

Untouchable fences! Immaculate chicken wire!
I shove my face against glass
recalling the shit and the choking
and the cyanide capsules dropping.
Their words were cattle prods.
Their photographs march forever in my brain
spoiling it. And the others
with bodies thinner than photographs
fall face down like lines of mannequins in my heart
spoiling it. Space

flares by . . . then face
after face face face face eyes
dizzy for creatures whizzing
and look! Angels
skipping down to hell for hell is lit
and light is laughter our eyes
don't laugh. Eyes! Laugh! Hug
this fear! Hug it!

Laughter hugs fear while angels gambol.
Creatures endow each other with beauty beauty
beauty beauty beauty beauty face
after face face face face face face face face where
are we going?

My grandma taught me how to kiss.
Like this she said
watch.
Wet gums my grandma had
and when she bit
snakes.

I smile a foolish smile.

Hate sits staring
and snaps my brain back.

Hate!
In your pants too death twits.
When the doors open
and it blows through like Lysol
your nose sniffs it too.
Most fertile compost pile.
Because it was so fouled.

So fouled with bones.
So fouled with hair.
With pounds and pounds of brain.
With miles of guts.
So fouled.
While the S.S. shadows that mess
stuffing gold nuggets into their teeth.

Hate!
When the lights go off
chills run between us
brother.

And once in Persephone's
garden below the porch I said
fuck.
Up above the females shook
and said and said and said and said
soap.

I smile my father's foolish smile.

Gargled out we snake
between buildings upward where Jesus saves.
A startle of pigeons crack my eyes up and Abraham
& Strauss say turn back.

The huge stones brood circled by silence.
The cables are tight veins beating into my heart.
The cables are swung from heaven
a carousel distant with angels and wings
and the harbor is sprung in my loins.

I whistle across water at Brooklyn Bridge.
Birds burst from my lips toward Brooklyn Bridge.
The setting sun hums on Brooklyn Bridge.
The horizon is an orchard there are camels
loaded with libraries donkeys
bearing melons and apples and grapefruit
an old lady giving birth to an orange and who
but a few poets and for one second some suicides
and a man lame with love to build that bridge?
And my throat is hoarse with such a need to shout
Look at that bridge just look at it!

The old buildings are blinking with proverbs.
Beauty is slitting to a close above us.
We vacuum back into darkness oh creature!

RAINY SUNDAY NIGHT, I LOOK AT
PHOTOGRAPHS ON THE WALL

There are times
I am lost in a shoe
four hundred feet
below the ground.

Inside
are people soft-shoeing silently.
Or eating.
Or staring hauntingly ahead.
These mirrors
multiply
our chewing jaws
infinitely.
In each room sits
my own death
with an egg in its hand.
I look away to the window.
A figure
leans forward trying to see in.
Whoever you are I would kiss your hands
and breathe gently in your hair
and touch my fingers to your lips.
Your breath

appears and dissolves on the glass
and behind it
a smile begins.

In my heart a zoo
heat of apes growling for oxygen
frozen hissings of tigers
frustration of mandrills biting glass
the lost bitterness of elephants begging
and always the highways dissipate
the slaughtered
echoings of butterflies in my temples.

Easy breathing
against my cheek.
You sleep
tingling in my daydreams.
I lean my body to yours quietly
A flowering ache breaks
spreading
your sluggish limbs apart,
gratefully my want becomes our love

Tacoma Cucamonga Salinas
Cheyenne Tuscaloosa Lake Champlaigne

Long hair I have
like a poet.
Big belly I have
like a man with a big belly watching television
and eating an apple
and eating a pear
and eating an orange
and sucking watermelon pits
and dreaming
of bunches of bananas
of bunches of grapes
of bunches of days
lost like the words and the tiny strangers
who falsely flit through your house each night
papa.

And Shira my daughter.
Gloomy Sunday night.
Tomorrow
we will ride to work
coffee taste still
sickening
and each of our pairs
of eyes
finding their own
empty space.

Death will come.

On Clove Road no light sweeps past.
Fogged sounds dissolve.
I am alone.
A flashlight pacifies me.

Tomorrow we will ride to work
our silence
in the turning wheels
desirable
as the blanket
when the cold morning
wakes us up.
The headlines
will slowly suck
our brains
into strange daydreamings.
Funeral business.

Washington Beaver Falls Monticello
Ogden Sault St. Marie Mohawk Valley
Beacon Saginaw Boston
our genius is dropping bombs.

Gloomy Sunday night
I'm out of words
and the radio
honoring the Sabbath
is whispering to me of Jesus Christ.

Turn it off. Turn it off.

I lie stomach-down
in a field
watching Queen Anne's lace cradling
and the breeze
touching my chest delights me
and my head
which rests like a large cocoon in my hands
is still.
I am lost on the giant planet of the spider.

The room
pierced
by sirens.
I lean to the window and look out.
Except
for the raindrops
the silence is unbroken.
Red lights glow.

Spring Street is slick
shining as far as I can see
as if
for each person looking out tonight
there's a separate street
each person
sucked through a tunnel
to a new life.

The darkness makes me feel sweet.
I give birth to an old man
who sits next to me on the train
telling me stories.
I think if I climbed into his ear
I would be soothed.

Father!
the fat loaves of bread cost more than I have.
My fingers are lean
teasing
each other
like long unwatered nerves.

Detroit Chicago New York City

Oh
I am in the confidence
of a short ancient god
whose one remaining power
is to enchant this lonely poet.

I turn back.
the room is turning over
the lightbulb hanging down
is a plant growing up
becoming sunlight.
The photographs on the wall
are like rapid sparks of raindrops in the puddle.

All night
we stare at death in each other's eyes
and the bread
must be broken
into a billion shares.

Look!
Ma Rainey's beautiful face
reminding me
of that face
when my eyes were closed
the smooth pillow

soothing
my cheek
all things alive
were grains of sand on my eyelids
their firm
slender
untouchable bodies
my young boy's desire
gagged
by sunlight
alone
in this tepid bed
in this cold coffin
my lips gently dreaming on your face
myself
disappearing
into
sleep.

Reminding me of Suzan.
And the flowering
of Suzan's
sadness
reminds me of Phyllis.
There she is
nursing our child.

Lips
do you remember her breasts?
Tongue
do you remember her milk?

Monhegan Island Fire Island Weehawken
Chattanooga Chataqua Selma Buffalo

And Billie Holiday smiling
And grandmother
so beautiful
young
I could make love to you
so old
like the torn stained couch covers.
And Hart Crane
to whom I made promises.
The vast ocean
pulls me.
And Mayakovsky
just about to explode.

And Billie Holiday smiling.

And my sister
plump

like a Russian pumpkin
now
dissolved
into house wifery.
And Shira my daughter.
And Theodore Roethke
his eyes popping from his saddened face
searching
his own death.
The vast ocean pulls me.

Pacific Atlantic Hudson
Tittebawasee Mississippi Missouri
Columbia Canada Greenland

I am the son of each one of you I look at now.
And Shira my daughter

And Jeriann
my wife
how alone your breathing is behind me.
All night
in the narrow bed
our bodies just touching
whenever you turn
I turn

on this slow swirling planet
covered by darkness.

I tell you
that the ground I fumble across
is part of a star
breaking
down
through the leaves
down
in jagged patches on the dark highway
down
into bright minerals
down
gently
on your nakedness
as you sleep dark child by the open window.

And there you are again
a baby
squeezed to your twin sister
in your father's arms
a young
shy man looking
somehow
smaller

than the baby daughters in his arms
looking
years later
like Pierrot.

And your mother.
A vase of flowers behind her
she toasts the air.
I remember her at the seashore
the water
above her chest
her chin thrust out
defiantly
yet
as lost looking as pieces of wood are
in the throttling
waves.

And strange fruit
hanging.

And Federico
of whom the poets speak
more beautiful than grass
the apple of our eye
and they killed him.

And Shira my daughter.
And Botts.
From nowhere you appear on a bridge.
From nowhere your poems slip into my heart.
And father.
Smiling for a photograph
your shirt
buttoned to the top
your face
a shy child's face
waiting
for death.

Beltz mein shtetele Beltz

You always sang that song
after supper
after supper
each night.
Where is Beltz?
Was it a good place to live in father?

And Billie Holiday smiling.

And Shira my daughter.
And mother

I tower above you
your bosom pushed plump to my belly.
I remember you
a woman whose deep voice
sang of Russia
that place where mothers come from
sang
of a man
who lived in a tree
because the tree was bare
and the man was a poet.

In the Greyhound terminal in Salt Lake City
there's an old man selling pillows.

Ellis Island
Staten Island Brownsville Williamsburg
Bensonhurst Fall River San Francisco

And there
again
you hold me around the waist
I am curlier
smaller
than you are Shira
yet your father.

You are as big as my big sister
who looms there
above me
all knowing
yet you are my daughter.
When morning comes I will go to visit you.

And beautiful Billie Holiday smiling.

Pittsburgh Black Rock Point Lobos
Point Reyes Santa Cruz Passaic
Little Bighorn Welfare Island Flatbush
Harlem Philadelphia Castroville
Mount Pisgah La Jolla Altoona
Yellowstone Paterson Downsville
Laredo Green Mountain Camden
Monterey Oswego Poughkeepsie
Vicksburg Chillicothe Cayuga
Vermillion Helena Denver
Coney Island Puget Sound Long Island Sound
Sandy Hook Coos Bay Wounded Knee

The moonlight reaching into your room
you are alone
you are pure
you are like a tree

you are the flat valley outside.

If I could make a pile of your crushed dreams it would
reach the moon.

And the Lord said
Sing Unto Me a New Song.

Going to see my daughter
bright October afternoon
the trees in the park are bare
the people are each alone.
The clouds are large and soft
the airplane looks make believe
the children's toys on the ground
are as large, each toy glistens
like a nose a stone a wet leaf
truck fire engine horse shovel

after it rains
the streets even in this city
smell fresh.

Going to see my daughter
it is summer
it is spring

it is autumn
it is winter
I walk briskly forward
she sees me coming toward her
on funny feet
how slender she looks
small child
as she was
through the doorcrack
her tininess
when I left the house for work each morning.

Oh we enter each other's darknesses
so brightly.

Going to see my daughter
carrying the faces of my life
with me
and through me they become
for you too
my child
beautiful.

Danang Bien Hoa Hei Phong
Quang Khe Xombang Dong Hoi
Vinh Lin Hanoi Hanoi Hanoi

Dyet ta oolitza
Dyet ta dum
Dyet ta borishka
shtuyer le blu.

Voota ta oolitza
Voota ta dum
Voota ta borishka
shtuyer le blu.

> Where is the street
> Where is the house
> Where is the small girl
> that I love.

> Here is the street
> Here is the house
> Here is the small girl
> that I love.

FROM DAY TO DAY

My own dwelling
is at night in
the space of your
breathing in the
borrowed time in
the crystals of
quartz in my hand
in a snapshot in
their nakedness in
the pellets of death
in the consultant
his ear to the wall
in soundless expiring
of oxygen in the
frozen plumbing in
the wrenched gold
fillings in the
sour taste of your
coins in your gray
thickness of cities
in my child asleep
in the napalm in her
fists in a village in

Vietnam in my mouth
of ashes in their
spread eagled spines
in a prophecy of
insects afflicting
my window in the
lonely space of your
breathing in your
separate being in
your woman's body
in your warmth in
our bed in the
borrowed time in
the rainfall easing
this darkness in
my own dwelling
in my own dwelling.

IN MEMORIAM

Footsteps that I take
each
one
stopped
by
stone
steps of my life
am I stepping to an execution?

Metallic
face
of the firing squad
your sockets
gleam
in my beating heart
you enter a church
fumbling
a question
of marriage
in your hands
you kneel
so that
your bullets

beat
straight
at my chest
a catastrophe of memories
a green wall
a blinding sun
a beating of a drum in my silence.

Union
Carbide
observes my terror
my eyes
tiny
prehistoric birds
hands
tied
behind my back
a sharp laugh
confuses
my hesitating steps
silence
prods my spine
I.B.M.
immaculately notes it.

They say you screamed
Federico García Lorca
I too will scream
because
the emptiness into which we gaze
the emptiness in their faces
is more terrible
than the emptiness that awaits.

This poem chokes in my heart
Lorca
beloved.

IN MY SILENCE

Either
it's raining
or the coffee
percolates
the words we speak
are invisible
are weightless
tonight
the cells of my body
are jagged
edges
the *New York Times*
old miseries
rain
comes
down
on the roof of my cabin
cold
rain
endlessly
children are born
sleep
on a mud floor

warm
body
I can taste
blades
of water
in your hair
your
salt
in my mouth
newspaper print dissolves
blackening
my taste buds.

Tonight
black
coffee
keeps me together
because
coffee is money
is heat on my fingertips
is utter poverty
is a cup
of oil
in which to snuff out
cigars
money smell not of people

it is
on this ground
they murder a fish peddler
for his politics
odor
of his clothes
everyone is a stranger
the words
we speak
is rainfall in my body
tonight
black
coffee
injures me.

BREATHING

I
one
from
silence
armed
with my heart
cry out.
This afternoon
the pond is almost empty
weeds
reach out
naked
barren
muffling sun
muffled
gray city sitting
on doorsteps
the cop's nightstick is wet
rubs
it
with his hand
I stomp in a field
the flies

follow
I sweat
I think napalm
no poems
I do not want to be me
a squat barn
aloof
a tank crushing
others
nothing essential between us
telephone
wires birds
armed
with my heart
no
words
between us
I wait
tonight
stars will remind me
child.

BOMBER'S MOON

The full moon
the edge
of a knife
illuminating the mist of this valley
and all people
standing
dark figures in a field
I cannot see their faces
my own face
tingles
sun
warms my stupor
oh
they *are* my sisters
my brothers
I cannot tell
one
from another
silence fills me with holes
the white barn
broken
gray city
broken bird on a road

we placed it in a box
bits of corn
scorched
bodies
the maple tree beside my cabin
our kindness
bits
of bread
Wall Street
your sunless granite greed
green money
What good are poems?
bits of bread for a dead child
as if I too would send yellow roses?

Illuminating
in the fingers of my right hand
all creatures
who cry in darkness
solid
everlasting
shapes of mountains
skull of a knife
dull
mindless
rhythms

of men marching
marching
laughter of women
echoes
of my own mortality
face of my child
breathing of all people at night
dark
figure
standing in a field
this light
illuminates
this planet
we haven't even learned to touch.
I accuse you Jerome
of desiring the moonlight.
I am angry at your inability to kill.

The Moon Oh The Moon The Moon
The Moon.

A DARKNESS BETWEEN US

A fly
a ceremony
of feet
on my ceiling
a man
a moonlit night
is dancing
stepping
along a path
to his house
a sniper
a blank
check
in his head
a motorcycle
inside
the lampshade
its buzz
is greater
than its world
anywhere
on any angle
is its bed

I watch it
walk on water
upside
down
from my own life
oh
this silent
flash
toward
nothing.

FOREVER

Forever
whistles
down
forever
turns
in your fists
forever
fingers
your heart
forever
explores
your intestines
forever
sits
on the cold ends
of your nerves
forever
locks
in your brain
forever
pictures
tumble
away

from you forever
cold
black
night
cold
black
rain
seeds
are unbearably
beautiful.

A BURNING COAL

Vulnerability
I hear
in my voice
saying
"is this for me?"
silences me
all evening.
Somewhere
someone
is saying
"is this for me?"
So much warmth
from an ash
mortality
fills me
with your face.

STILL AWAKE AT DAWN I LOOK OUT

1.
It will rain all day
gray
puppet
strings
a pair of long underpants
an old man
sways
heavily
in the dim dawn light
my brain
is a casket
tapped
upon
by raindrops
oh
that you are able
to pucker your life
into a kiss
fills my face with a grin
you
are
still

sleeping
all your queerness
tucked in
with you.

2.
Each
day
we communicate
with
Standard
Oil
soaking
our bread
in their gasoline
empty
oil
drums
now
are filling with rainwater
a goat
pokes
for leftovers
even
louder

than before
I see you
looking down at the pavement
your
jaw
full of coins
your fists of pebbles
eyes of rainfall
a turtle
just being stepped on
you
devastate
me
more
than my fear of death.

3.
Outside
sparrows are busily awake
no
taller
than abandoned beer cans
each
day
they must eat

twice
their own weight
they
bathe
furiously
joyously in the puddles
the drizzle
falling
closes my eyelids
go to sleep
later
you can write
now
sleep
you need sleep.

YOUR MOTHER KILLED IN A CAR CRASH

You see her body
the blood
sucked
from her mangled flesh
a clean corpse
horrible music
dim blue lights
a dead womb
inside a dead body
inside a bronze box
your womb
from which you have been taken
your flesh
therefore
dead
your
mystery
sucked from your eyes
there's no way
to cover
over
your heart your mama
is dead

child
the box is open
all see the inside of your womb
and it is nothing now
except
in your dreams at night a few more years.

HUSBAND
(for Lewie Meyers)

In Michigan Union basement grill
you suck your coffee down
and you count the length of a line
both by its vowels and those "grave toys"
leftover from hot-water flats in Washington
> (where heavy pillows are covered with dead flowers
> upon which the shadows of aunts and uncles
> are stains).

I think of you sitting in class with a frown
as private as your own birth
> or your own funeral,
until the teacher says:
> "will the saturnine young man in the back
> open the window please"
Your stark hands
lean out from black tight wool.

You said no matter what poems you make about your wife
you never *get* her out of bed.

As for me,

       for whom the long heat of her hands
       are distant as a dream I used to have
       in my family's wallpapered apartment in Brooklyn),
I remember you sitting your usual
in the Union one day
       and then your smile,
as she walked in,
       which said simply:
       I love you and you are my wife.

POETRY ALONG STATE STREET

Magnolias startle the ground three times each year.
And in winter the hail comes down.

Last Sunday afternoon it hailed
and all the bells in town rang like marbles in a bag.
I was in the street then
and when I unmuffled the sound of the bells
my throat leaped with an alien breath
of smoky boys pitching pellets down
to shut in tight the wonder of eyes
and put the knowledge of an ancient desert on my cheeks.

But there were no boys.
For when I tried again the bells were silent
and curving in, in the sky, was a veritable universe of falling,
flicking fast to a vision of trees.

I thought of Labrador where the world is wet
and then of Tibet where trees are speechless.
For the petrified trees were in bloom
and each was a snowflake pulling in the day.

A BILLION MILES TO MAKE LOVE

A black butterfly
against the kiosk on Union Square
struggles to fly off.

"García Lorca," my friend whispers.

DECEMBER MORNING ON THE BOARDWALK

Sitting side by side
sunlight
seizes their faces
the old woman
shivering
in the sea wind in Coney Island
sucking
sunlight
from the ocean
wanting to live and live and live.

LATE NIGHT FOOTSTEPS ON THE STAIRCASE

Hey
you!
break down my door and say something
I won't be silent or huffy or heavy
I'll prance on the tips of my toes a happy ape
who's learned to speak
alphabets will stick in my beard
and shake free and scatter
we'll whistle tunes from our lips
and those tunes will slow down
to the wheat field whispers of our flesh

All night long
I have thought about you America
in darkness
your deeds

Long live a hunger to feed each other.

ACKNOWLEDGEMENTS

The publication of *Long Live a Hunger to Feed Each Other* is the result of the sustained determination and effort of Jeri Hilderley.

It is also made possible by the donation in 1995 of Badanes's papers to the University of Michigan Library by Gail Kinn; the acceptance and care of his papers at the library by Kathryn Beam and Kathleen Dow; and the ongoing commitment to Badanes's work by Thomas Beller.

This publication is supported in part through the generosity of the following individuals: Edward Botts, Marianne Burke, Dorien Grunbaum, Jeri Hilderley, Paul Hollister, Carol Japha, Gail Kinn, Ellen Kozak, Eric Lindbloom, James Lindbloom, Judith Lindbloom, Gilbert Levin, Paul Russell, and Nancy Willard.

Also from Open City Books,
available at bookstores nationwide and at
www.opencity.org:

Actual Air: Poems by David Berman

Venus Drive: Stories by Sam Lipsyte

My Misspent Youth: Essays by Meghan Daum

World on Fire by Michael Brownstein

Karoo: A Novel by Steve Tesich

Goodbye, Goodness: A Novel by Sam Brumbaugh

The First Hurt: Stories by Rachel Sherman

Some Hope: A Trilogy by Edward St. Aubyn

Mother's Milk: A Novel by Edward St. Aubyn

Love Without: Stories by Jerry Stahl